B. Point Publishing

presents

Unfinished Business:

Letters to a Broken Me

a poetry book

By: Bee Maree

Copyright

Other Titles by Poet:

Tense: Journey of an Unknown

Poet

Table of Contents

a collection of poetic-diary

filled letters

Acknowledgement

To: Christiana, Eugene', Tiffany and Zakia.

I most certainly must take the time to recognize these four beautiful souls who have helped contribute to my book by offering beautiful pieces specifically written by my request. You guys are extremely dear to me and at some point, in my world you've made a vast difference. Thank you all; not only for this small contribution, but for the biggest ones you've made along the way with just your friendships. I love you all dearly.

Eugene'-

You're more than just a friend, you're family.

I chose "Becoming" because over the course of the years I have seen you transition and BECOME the woman you've worked so hard to grow into, so this was only fitting. The mom, the friend, the BOSS. I am so proud of you and only wish you the best. The path to great things has just begun and when it starts to curve, just keep going.

Zakia-

You found inspiration in me when I found it in you. Thank you for inspiring me and reminding me to continue to go after my passion.

I chose "Renew" because your transition hasn't been easy. Although, our time knowing each other has been short the impact your beauty inside and out has had is like no other. You're so passionate and resilient. You've faced many things unspoken of and still manage to achieve every goal you set your mind to. You've shown courage, strength, and tenacity.

You've found self-love and the power to wield your gifts and help others along the way and that selflessness alone deserves an applaud. You may not know but your presence, conversations and support has taught me much and I will forever appreciate you.

Christiana-

15 years of friendship couldn't make us closer.

I chose "fragments" because unlike most I've seen the hidden parts of you. The parts that have required strength to be pulled from under your feet to make way. I've seen what has looked like defeat covered in grace. I've seen tears that spelled out P.U.S.H and smiles that have hidden pain and fear. I've seen all these beautiful fragments come together to paint your picture: clear; brush strokes that blended well and left room for error.

You've continued to push me; you continue to believe in me, and I really can't see a single project that I produced not including you in some form. Thank you for always being here for me. In more ways than I could ever repay you for. I've seen a reflection of human. And our connection, no matter how far, or how long we go without speaking is forever. My other human. My forever person, I love you.

Tiffany -

My fun-size cousin. My personal assistant when needed, and friend. You came into my life at the most difficult stage of transition for me. While still learning and growing. 5 years later you are still apart of those lessons and growth. So, I guess you're stuck with me.

I chose "under" because no matter what low you've seen you've always risen above it. Under-valued, and unrewarded but still understanding. Selfless, compassionate, and always willing to see others around you rise. The energy you've presented with me will always be welcomed. As you've seen me through other accomplishments, I am pleased to have you be a part of this as well. I love you cousin and just know this is only one of many features to come.

To You-

    A special thanks to the one who resides in my beat. Although, no word was given to you it is the only one that I can place value on because it is where you will always be. No matter the road this journey has taken us on these lessons have definitely contributed to my growth and I can only express my gratitude from a sincere place. Our paths have taken us to different places but my well wishes to you are forever. You've certainly left a mark on me and I can only hope that I have done the same for you.

Love Always and Forever,

Bee

Dedication

Dear Me...

    Broken,

        Braised

            Bruised,

                Brittle,

                    Becoming

        Me...

I have gone over in my head a million times as to how I would write to you. How I would address this letter in telling you that after being through so much together how I only wish the best for you and congrats on all that you have overcome and have yet to accomplish.

But instead,

Unfinished Business: Letters to a Broken Me

All I want to say is …

Dear Broken Me:

We have unfinished business!

Warning

Stop!

I'm in my feelings ...

With no way to describe them

No escape to contain the way I feel

inside

so I lie to me

Tell myself I'm okay

To keep a smile on my face

While

Wheeling out of control

Spiraling into a hole

Deep Inside of my head

Feeding all of my insecurities

Dear Me

"it was time, trouble & trauma that allowed me to process all of my lessons learned from you"

<u>Feature</u>

Becoming By: Eugene' Jackson

Becoming

Who I am

Who TF am I?

I ask all the time

Are the answers in the stars in the sky?

Do I belong?

something isn't right

Becoming

who I am

Looking

Searching

Find Me

Are u inside

I'm knocking

Becoming who I am

Determined to find u

The obstacles inside u

Nothing will stop

Becoming who I am

The Darkness is it u

I will not let u in

I will not become

What is inside me

I refuse to allow u to

Become who I am

What I am

Beautiful

Genuine

Loyal

Determined

Loved

Appreciated

Undefeated

Will Eat U Alive

Is That Me?

Becoming

Not becoming...

Already

Became

hope:
hōp/

**1. a feeling of expectation and desire
for a certain thing to happen.**

"I <u>HOPE</u> you can hear me"

1. Hope

Dear Hope,

you never once let it wither away,

you believed in it every day

the very thing that the made you stay

through lies that lead to heartbreaks

and the world worked so hard to take from you

tried to wash away the very thing that was useful

this is how you made it out alive

you never let it out of your sight

the way you carved strength by just belief

is everything you gave to me.

Thank you.

de·sire
də ˈzī(ə)r/

1. strongly wish for or want (something).

"My <u>DESIRE</u> for you left me empty."

2. Desire

Dear Desire,

your appetite for pain increased

night after night hanging on to pieces of

promises left incomplete

wishing wells over flooded with salt-filled weeps

clinching to once satin-shared sheets

as you poured out silent screams through your

dreams

paralyzed with emotions

that sunk you ocean deep

impulse for love always kept you weak.

love
ləv/

1. an intense feeling of deep affection.

"My <u>LOVE</u> for you was limit-less."

3. Love

Dear Love,

It was the idea that you existed

That made it hard for me to resist it

The fact that someone could find it in their realm

to have that much affection

for me

So much that one could become the air

that I breathe

You gave me an attachment

One that I was able to hold a grasp of

That conveyed it was mine for the keeping

Although time showed a different meaning

No matter what

I never stopped believing

Unfinished Business: Letters to a Broken Me

Broken shell and insecurities

Never stopped my heart from beating

pain
pān/

1. **physical suffering or discomfort caused by illness or injury.**

"My heart was conditioned to <u>PAIN.</u>"

4. Pain

Dear Pain,

I hunted for you

Especially on the days where dark skies clouded my view

When my expectations went above standard

And I was left stranded

I waited in the dark for you to show up

Anticipating your arrival

Eyes filled with love

Just so you could snatch the voice that spoke so

delicately of it

So you could rush through my veins

Like a drug habit

I needed you

Unfinished Business: Letters to a Broken Me

I needed to feel that same hit I've been chasing

since I first met

What love felt like

I needed to feel broken

Because it was the only way that I could reel

back into motion

Sulk around the house where I'd be noticed

Just for another temporary moment

You allowed me to feel whole again

in·spi·ra·tion
/ˌinspəˈrāSH(ə)n/

1. the process of being mentally
stimulated to do or feel something, to
do something creative.

"It was your uncertainty that allowed my

INSPIRATION to grow."

5. Inspiration

Dear Inspiration,

You made me see myself

in a different light

I saw things through your eyes

For a change

Dancing to the music that you helped me to tune

into

Forgetting that I could dance

I dipped my feet into the ink and slid them right

across the lines

Spelling out the two-step as you showed me how

to glide

You ignited me

Ideas started to flow from my feet

Unfinished Business: Letters to a Broken Me

and we made beautiful work together by the tap

of the quill

Gripped so tightly

between our toes as we let the

calligraphy encrypt the music to no end

You reminded me

that the curves of the script were just the

beginning

Your influence pushed me forward and

helped me to write again

re·gret
/rə'gret/

1. feel sad, repentant, or disappointed over (something that has happened or been done, especially a loss or missed opportunity).

"My only <u>REGRET</u> was not loving you

through the moments I hated you."

6. Regret

Dear Regret,

You encouraged me to lose myself in the turmoil

You dampened my every moment to misery

Scissoring my heart at your leisure

Allowing me to do everything to please her

Carving intricate wounds inside my mind

Leaving streaks from tears screeching

down my face

That jumped across my water line

You planned every moment of this

Enjoying me groveling

in desperation at your test

No matter the consequence

I was your pawn in defense

dark·ness

/ˈdärknəs/

1. the partial or total absence of light.

"Your sudden departure led me to

DARKNESS."

7. Darkness

Dear Darkness,

I succumbed to your weakness

 in my most vulnerable moment

Let you blind me emotionless

in exchange

for a broken heart

Made a deal with your contract

and blackened my soul

All in an attempt

to make me whole.

in·no·cence

/ˈinəsəns/

1. lack of guile or corruption; purity.

"Stealing my INNOCENCE only pushed

me to go harder."

8. Innocence

Dear Innocence,

It was in your eyes that they believed you

Peering through your soul and knowing

immediately

You were just a petal of hope

Hoping for someone to love you,

approve of you

Be proud of you ,

hell,

anything you.

The call for lap dances,

and prancing fingers would know nothing of your

innocence

Had the call for your innocence not been ranged

Unfinished Business: Letters to a Broken Me

Had the trusted dialer not press the buttons

And your buttons not be the ones to come loose

Had your matured bosom not tempted the trusted

goose.

Maybe just maybe you could have saved her too

But before you could open your lips

The insert into your lips silenced you

Forbidding you to tell the truth

Oh, innocence

I'm sorry I was too late to save you.

De·cem·ber

/dəˈsembər/

1. the twelfth month of the year, in
the northern hemisphere usually
considered the first month of
winter.

"Born in a **DECEMBER** light taught me

how to battle the coldest encounters."

9. December

Dear December,

It was 7:47 PM; on a cold winter night that you

decided it was time.

Time to let a premature

3lb, 3 ½ oz melanated infant into the world

 to a mother

14 days under gauze and beeps

from the medical team's slumber

Feeding tubes and baby lube applied to stabilize

her

Oh, and how beautiful she would grow to be

Tiny but filled with

strength and certainty

Capricorn built so her personality hooved around

Unfinished Business: Letters to a Broken Me

Just as it was meant to be

Blessing the world with her presence

as the bayou weather sought her energy.

im·paired

/im'perd/

1. weakened or damaged.

"Broken promises **IMPAIRED** my

heart."

10. Impaired

Dear Impaired,

You shifted your weight time and time again

With countless trials to no end

All in the name of

Feeling.

With constant emotions reeling

Over

the meaningless

False facades of happiness

That led to trails of hearts left beat-less

Dreams turned to nightmares

Traded replacement smiles with fears

Weakened

The soul

Unfinished Business: Letters to a Broken Me

All along believed in your story told

Disguised as love

But turned out to be just another

damaged soul.

sub·stance

/ˈsəbstəns/

1. the quality of being important, valid, or significant

"What hurt the most is that I was

of no <u>SUBSTANCE</u> to you."

11. Substance

Dear Substance,

Where I should have looked for substance

I instead

accepted stupidity

Traded in common trauma bonds

mistaken for compatibility

Dabbled in your directory

only to end up short handed with missing digits

Shedded silent tears

with a heart that beated for unreturned love

Endlessly.

Dear You

"Word of Advice: It doesn't get easier, you just learn to master it better; No matter what,

YOU DO NOT GIVE UP!"

<u>Feature</u>

Fragments by Author Christiana Harrell

I wonder how you sleep at night

Do you awaken to the joy you found in my agony?

Was it fun for you to be the one with the gun?

The disillusioned power it brings to cowards that can't simply use their fist

Or their words

Honesty seemed too complicated a task

Maybe too much to ask… of you… from you

So, it'll seem drastic when I can only
imagine my suffering equal to being shot

Equal to never being able to return to who I
once was before your eyes were on me

Your arms around me

Your trauma inside me

I live with the fragments of your bullets

Your audacity

Your inability to love… yourself

in·se·cu·ri·ty

/ˌinsəˈkyŏŏrədē/

1. uncertainty or anxiety about oneself;
lack of confidence.

"Your failed promises over again; made

room for my **INSECURITIES.**"

12. Insecurity

Dear Insecurity,

how do I ensure that every moment will last with

you?

and that somewhere out of the blue

I won't be staring at the bottom pit

of an empty bottle,

swallowing

my heartaches

trying to numb the last few hours

That crashed and burned

with reactions from your actions

that stemmed from half-ass cowardly attempts to

assassin

My love for you

Unfinished Business: Letters to a Broken Me

How can I be assured that you won't pull that

same

"I'm into you, but it's' not you" line

That I've heard so many times

Only to end up admitting you don't want me

Can you please spare me the bullshit,

And remove me from this substitute position

If this isn't real.

ad·dic·tion

/əˈdikSH(ə)n/

1. the fact or condition of being addicted to a particular substance, thing, or activity.

"My <u>ADDICTION</u> grew for you with every

"I love you".

13. Addiction

Dear Addiction,

I can't quite pin

the first time

I said

this is it

The way it settled in my blood

that kept me open for another hit

The warm rush through my veins

And shiver down my back

The taste of the words that drip down my throat

As I whispered

I

love

you.

stand·ard

/ˈstandərd/

1. a level of quality or attainment.

"I was mistaken to think you fit the

STANDARD."

14. Lowe Standard

Dear Standard,

Damn, is that all that it took for you to be gone?
From your trip,
to my trip on less messages and no phone calls
Guess it seemed that my suspicions were right
all along
You'd reel me in just enough to bring me high
But what I couldn't see was the true Lowe
I know that disappointments come in many forms
But I was hoping you'd be the one to prove me
wrong
I wasn't looking for you to feed me stories or
apolo-LIE
But at least be accountable, you knew the shit
that you were doing wasn't right
How the routine switched up over the course of a
night
And despite my efforts to let it ride

My intuition only brought about raised eyebrows

And instant regret

That I let your energy enter my space and

allowed you to part between my legs

That my expectations grew with the "baes" and

every night that we slept

Fuck wrong with me, not like I was in love yet.

I wasn't in love with you

But I definitely cared.

And after belting out my worries

You left it right there

Not a conversation more could have made the

confirmation any clearer

Shifted my standards to accept you

Knowing that the flags were red

su·gar rush

1. a sudden and brief burst of energy supposedly experienced after the consumption of food or drink with a high sugar content.

"You were my <u>SUGAR-RUSH</u>."

15. Sugar Rush

Dear Sugar-Rush,

I chuckle at the thought that you think that I'm

sweet

But the reality is that the taste of my nectar will

leave your thoughts beat….

Weak

And restless

Sitting next to my shell and you still won't be able

to pass the test

Because….

It's difficult

This code to my soul has no combination

My laughter is only present to tease your

sensations

Unfinished Business: Letters to a Broken Me

My eyes will only confuse your senses...

Like

Did you taste what I said?

Or

Did you hear how that felt?

You won't even be able to decipher the difference

Mainly because you're too high for this shit

That when the gears shift

You will no longer have control of where this

ends

Or connects

My fingertips caressing your back

Alleviating inflamed tension

And pressure cracks

Following the trail through your locks

Unfinished Business: Letters to a Broken Me

Now I'm trapped

Fuck

rewind that back

Don't do that

How you reel me into comfort

When I'm a nervous wreck

You leave me with ill ease

But I'm still lookin' for the bite

from that dog ass nigga's teeth

Clinching everything about me

that the world doesn't see

Peeling layers of disappointments and broken

promises

just to lay with me

Never thought taking time with you

Unfinished Business: Letters to a Broken Me

would allow me to find peace.

envy

/ˈenvē/

1. a feeling of discontented or resentful longing aroused by someone else's possessions, qualities, or luck.

"Your position was never mine to <u>ENVY</u>,

yet I still did"

16. Envy

Dear Envy,

I've grown impatient

With battered soles

And aching bones

Tell me

How much longer

do I have to sit here waiting

While my eyes celebrate others wins

and timelines stating

"Congratulations"

But,

where's my acclamation

As I drag from sun-up to sun-down

Just barely making it

Over-exerting my power

Just to extend to another day

Burnt out on prayers and the idea that

What's for me

is on the way.

po·et·ry

/ˈpōətrē/
1. literary work in which special intensity is given to the expression of feelings and ideas by the use of distinctive style and rhythm; poems collectively or as a genre of literature.

"**<u>POETRY</u>** has always been my weapon

of choice"

17. Poetry

Dear Poetry,

I found my voice with you

Through crooked lines and scripted rhymes

I found a way to release

To Break free

from bounds and chains

That kept me hung

Silencers that kept me hushed

while the pain built up

It was through your rhythm and flow that I could

finally speak

Easy with the pen to the sheet

Everything that was me

Became you

Unfinished Business: Letters to a Broken Me

with

Lines of free verse and haikus

So vivid you could see the imagery

I brought you to the stationary just so I could

defeat the enemy

You've held me up when it felt like the walls were

caving in

and my back were against it

I will never forget

how you've always

been a friend to me.

con·fir·ma·tion

/ˌkänfərˈmāSH(ə)n/

1. the action of confirming something
or the state of being confirmed.

"It was through your silence and lack of

action that I found <u>CONFIRMATION </u>the

most."

18. Confirmation

Dear Confirmation,

I wondered for awhile

what the truth would feel like

Surprisingly,

no different

from the same lips that parted

and spoke lies

Each word,

confirmation

for what I already visualized

Although it brought tears to my eyes

it was my soul

that screamed from the inside

That's what broke me down.

be·com·ing

/bəˈkəmiNG/

1. the process of coming to be
something or of passing into a state

"I can no longer let your love stand in

the way of who I am BECOMING"

19. Becoming

Dear Becoming,

Becoming…

Something I channel so often

when did I become the me that excused bullshit

for loving

So forgiving…

So oblivious

to smack dab in my face

So me

So big-hearted

So understanding

So much "I give a damn because no one ever

took the time to show you what love is"

When did I designate

Unfinished Business: Letters to a Broken Me

myself as the savior

Trading in my heart for a few "I love you's"

that really didn't mean anything when you said it

Becoming...

The proud me

but still shelling insecurities

Still sticking around

While you keep me down

Still trying to become

one with you

Dreams of forever that'll never come true

Just still chasing

Yesterday's cravings

Beating pavements that led to dead end

engagements

Unfinished Business: Letters to a Broken Me

All while hoping that

we can still make it

dis·ap·point·ment

/ˌdisəˈpointmənt/

1. sadness or displeasure caused by the nonfulfillment of one's hopes or expectations

"My constant belief in you kept me

<u>DISAPPOINTED</u>"

20. Disappointment

Dear Disappointment,

I don't hate you

The problem is

that I love you so much

And no matter how we add it up

divide or multiple

We're never gonna solve the sum

Do you know how many nights

I've waited for you to fight

To scoop the spare key from under the rug

And make your way in from the night

But ,

you never came through to make amends

Instead you flexed with your friends

And took day trips with that bitch

But what did she do to deserve this?

Besides stepping on toes with an already landed

agenda

Manic personality

With manipulation that pulled the trigger

Of tall lies and fake cries

Now you figure you can fix her?

Feeling sorry and excusing the behavior

all because you didn't want to "hurt her"

or see it end

Shit is so crazy...

How did you ever allow yourself to fall

"fall in" this deep

With false hopes and family plans of what you

thought it could be

Now I'm expected to let it roll and just accept

reality?

Heart broken in my palm

Steady got me questioning

How could you let the days roll by

Unfinished Business: Letters to a Broken Me

and NOT think of me

rage
[rāj]

1. violent, uncontrollable anger

"I have yet to release <u>RAGE</u> on you.

21. Rage

Dear Rage,

I tried

to keep you bottled up

So that I would never have to show this side

Fear

Of not knowing

Your strength

Your wits

No matter how hard I tried

My thoughts were

never fit to contain you

trust
[trəst]

1. firm belief in the reliability, truth, ability, or strength of someone or something.

"My lack of <u>TRUST</u> never stopped me

from loving you"

22. Trust

Dear Trust,

I remember the first time I laid eyes on your

deceit

It dripped with disguise that you loved me

Wrapped tightly in promises

And planted venom-like kisses

of tales that I often yearned to miss

I held on to the hope

Pretending it kept me warm

Afraid of letting go

so I turned a blind eye

just so I could go home to it

Climb into bed and snuggle up to the foolery

Excused the mishandled manner

Unfinished Business: Letters to a Broken Me

Allowed you to make a fool of me

Defended your abandonment

Only to end up bedside stranded

Just so that I could cry tears

that proved to you

 I deserve this.

Dear World

"Preparing for you has been my biggest feat, yet; I AM READY!"

Feature

By: Zakia Stewart

When I think of Renew
I think of my life
Growing up thinking I'm going to be someone's
wife

Young child so innocent not knowing about the
life planned ahead
Going from house to house not knowing when
I'm ever gonna get my own bed

Days pass, long nights
Knowing he had no rights

Touching in places that shouldn't be touched
As he clutched my waist

It's an unexplainable feeling knowing you can't
tell a soul
Knowing that I wasn't in control

Came from a broken home
Where I was feeling alone

Late nights drinking hard

Unfinished Business: Letters to a Broken Me

Who is the man; supposed to be a father figure

Went from sweet hugs, to violent throws
All because he wanted hoes

Not realizing he had a beautiful queen that cooks
& cleans

Mother of four
He continues to hurt her to her core

I never knew pain
But I knew I had more to gain

A part of me died a part I could never access
again
It's like a casket

This moment that forever changed how I saw the
world
I couldn't believe it my head was on swirl

Forever changed my ability to be that innocent &
carefree
But it looks like this how it had to be

I'm dealing with the curse attached to the casket
Feeling like a heavy basket

Unfinished Business: Letters to a Broken Me

In the middle of the pain was a promise that god
inserted
I had to keep going even if it hurt

I'm grateful for my teachers who saw something
in me when I couldn't see it myself
Created an environment for me to flourish when I
felt like I was dying

I'm breaking that generational curse
So things get better not worse

I'm going to kill some things so that my kids
never have to do it again
I know what it's like crying myself to sleep

I decided that will be the only tears that women
cry who are connected to me
I will be the key

I came to stir up the gift god gave me down in the
inside
I will no longer hide

I'm here for the little girl who lost her dreams
I'm going to be shining so bright it's going to be
like a beam
You're telling me give up and that makes me go
stronger

Unfinished Business: Letters to a Broken Me

Only to unleash the hunger

You're telling me back down makes me worship
even more
And I would kindly show you the door

I came here to be a redeemer for everything
connected to me
I'm not stopping until you see

I have a purpose attached to me
So I will choose to be free

I'm going to war with the devil I'm sorry but I
wouldn't be me unless I go to war
Baby I'm knocking at his door

I believe in a healer whom couldn't be more
realer

You can tell me it's over that's alright because he
starts things all over again he makes all things
new
So don't look blue when I come through

After life had knocked me down I had to get back
up
I will not let depression ever come back closeup

Unfinished Business: Letters to a Broken Me

My spirt is returning
I see my life turning

No weapon formed against me will prosper
I'm a king's daughter

There's been has been a crown attached to my
head
No more tears will I shed

He kept me alive so I can be a testimony to
everyone attached to me
So, I had to agree
For so long my life was on pause
Because I was stuck on my flaws
ITS TIME I RENEW MY JOURNEY

tox·ic

/ˈtäksik/

1. very harmful or unpleasant in a pervasive or insidious way.

"My heart was fueled by your <u>TOXIC</u>

ways"

23. Dear Toxic

Dear Toxic,

I knew it was a lie when I said it

Through streaming tears and clenched teeth

I instantly regretted

I kept the gateway opened so you could

trespass

Kept my availability clear to schedule

uncomfortable meetings

Just so I could get a glimpse at

You

All so my anxiety could run through

Followed by screams that belted out why's, leave

me "alone's" and fuck you's

When I really didn't want to

Unfinished Business: Letters to a Broken Me

Just so I could create what appeared to be

unwanted dialogue

And push you to leave the room

Quickly responded to heart racing messages

With little to no effort

Trying to hold on to memories of what use to be,

us

Still anticipating the moment you'd realize it's

time to give the bullshit up

Expecting you to give me, me

But it ain't no trust

Time and time again you took my choices away

You were doing too much

So much pain built up Inside

Yet I still yearned for your touch

Unfinished Business: Letters to a Broken Me

That I could only muster the energy to say

I hate you

In exchange for love

bro·ken

/ˈbrōkən/

(of a person) having given up all hope;
despairing.

"I showed up for you even when you left

me **BROKEN**."

24.Chard Love (Broken)

Dear Broken,

So funny to think that you could love me when

you were so broken...

Offering fragments of what I thought was whole

So, I put my heart on pause

and kept that space open

Hoping

That one day you would see

That you issued more pain than love

in exchange for momentary....

For slighted eyes and tongues that whispered of

small fantasies

In the midst of our storm, it was easy to whisk

you away from me

And I'll take that

You were so stuck on what you lost in the old me

you didn't notice that you got an upgrade in the

process

Going back-to-back

You have habits like an addict

So you are forever on a journey

still chasing that very first hit

Reclining back

Lightin' up the pipe

For a release from reality

Over and over

Feeding false hopes of what I thought was meant

to be

Revolving memories

while you get to flex with no penalties

Now I'm picking myself apart battling self-regret

and insecurities

I just hate the fact

That I ever let you get

that close to me

ab·sence

/ˈabsəns/

1. the state of being away from a place or person.

"In my <u>ABSENCE</u> your heart will ache as

I did when you were present"

25. Absence

Dear Absence,

You're gonna love me in ways

that you've never known

Place me on top

when you're in the wrong

Grovel on ground

just to come home

You'll love me most

when I'm gone

com·mit·ment
/kə'mitmənt/

**1. the state or quality of being
dedicated to a cause, activity, etc.**

"My <u>COMMITMENT</u> to you was

supposed to be forever"

26. Commitment

You say you're stepping to the plate

with intentions to commit.

But the question that lies open is,

"are you done with all of your shit?"

Have you unloved all of the others that have

come before me?

Or am I here to heal the wounds that are still

fresh and bleeding

Become your punching bag in the night

when you have to face reality

So, you shuffle me back through the deck

Realizing you aren't ready for me

change
[CHānj]

1. make (someone or something) different; alter or modify

"One day I will <u>CHANGE</u> the world."

27. Change

Dear Change,

I wanna see change

I wanna be the range

of clouds from each ends of the earth

Birthing

new mindsets

that test the societal values that we constantly

conform to

because this is all that we know

I want better goals

I'm still challenging you to hold

the hand of that brown skin girl

and never let it go

She needs guidance

Unfinished Business: Letters to a Broken Me

she needs reminders

we need hope

their future is our role,

accountable for their strolls

through each step

skip, jump and hop

through tire holes

battered staircases,

tripping down sidewalk pavements

lighting their dark moments

when it seems that they won't make it

I wanna see change

so I'm starting with what's in front of me

my 4c patterned haired beauties

because they look up with wide brown eyes

Unfinished Business: Letters to a Broken Me

even after tears cried

and still expect me to save the day

still trusting my stern tone

and push for greatness

they need me

they need us

to lean on the shoulder of love

when nothing else makes sense

when it seems like everything is going to shit

just know that doing it for them

we are their "win"

bind·ing

/ˈbīndiNG/

1. the action of fastening or holding together, or of being linked by chemical bonds.

"The <u>BINDING</u> was never thick enough

to keep us together"

28. Binding

Dear Binding,

I used to believe that love healed everything

That simple "I love you's" validated mistakes

made

and reinforced the "unconditional" love statement

That tight hugs at night and pulling you closer

meant comfort

Followed by forehead kisses that put you to

slumber

That cycling back around said you were

choosing" me over her

That believing lies told covered up the bullshit

and the hurt

That bigger gifts and small promises kept

Unfinished Business: Letters to a Broken Me

Meant that our love was strong

That showing up despite the matter would prove

that I was the one

Never noticed all the while these triggers kept me

confined to our potential

That eventually we'd get it right and put to rest

the constant tussle

No matter what right or wrong time would prove

to wounds that healed

Only to expose that all the while

The love that kept me bonded

Wasn't real.

naked
[ˈnākid]

1. (of something such as feelings or behavior) undisguised; blatant

"You've always laid out the <u>NAKED</u>

truth; it was necessary"

29. Naked

Dear Naked,

You attempted to strip me bare

Just so that you could see

Traced my scars like dotted braille lines

Because it was the only way that you could read

me

Grazed your fingertips across the nape of my

neck

Gripping locks of hair by the seams

Whispered sweet nothings upon my ears

Just so that you could peer into my dreams

Strolled my shoulder blade walkway

Traveled thorough my crooked spine

Fell deeply into the dips of my lower bottom line

Drew me close into your arms and cupped my

curves without a sign

Reassured my insecurities with parted lips that

spoke of "time"

Faced my bare cheeks head on

Placed your hands upon my chest

Counted the beats my heart would take until it

came to rest

You left a mark upon my soul that forced me to

face the truth

Never knew being so vulnerable would allow me

to lend my heart to you

despair
[dəˈsper]

1. the complete loss or absence of hope.

"I never thought losing you would send

me into <u>DESPAIR</u>".

30. Despair

Dear Despair,

I just

wanted to let my hair down

And subsequently,

release me of all the toxins and the problems that

my stress found

Comb through the strands of damage ends

With wide tooth combs big enough to separate

my battered feelings

Condition the minerals to restore strength

Massage oils throughout the follicles to protect

my heart's shield

Mold and brush the side burns of pain

Only to sever ties by the blade of shears

To alleviate me of this dead weight

ef·fort

/ˈefərt/

1. a vigorous or determined attempt.

"The <u>EFFORT</u> put forth will always stand out to me"

31. Effort

Dear Effort,

I laid out the means to access

And told the promising

she had to earn me

She shifted her eyes about the word

So I shifted my thoughts about this bird

Because

I said it right the first time

Earn me

Expect nothing but what you see

And work to gain everything that is me

Give me the same energy you seek

Unfinished Business: Letters to a Broken Me

Time is valuable

The hands of the clock do not tick for our

enjoyment

It winds down every experience

because time is only borrowed

Yet

We spend its moments

Disintegrating

Simply surviving

With no rhyme or reason

Just breathing

be·lief

/bə ˈlēf/

1. trust, faith, or confidence in someone or something.

"My <u>BELIEF</u> in you cost me more

in the end."

32. Belief

Dear Belief,

I just wanted to trust in you

Be reassured

that you have every intention to do right

Not just because

I'm right

But

because you want it

Want me

Unconditionally,

By your side

Battling your pride

Baring humility

in the heat of the moment

Owning it

Trusting you to shield me with protection

With hopes I lowered my guards

again

just so you could accept me.

clo·sure

/ˈklōZHər/

1. a sense of resolution or conclusion at the end of an artistic work.

"The only <u>CLOSURE</u> I ever needed from

you was to let me go."

33. Closure

Dear Closure,

My heart

prayed for this moment

Where my loyalty and love

could be extracted from the brokenness

escape your hold

that kept me complacent in time

lifted the seals from my lips

And from my eyes the fold-blind

Begged for the day my leash would become

detached from your grip

And my eagerness to show up for you

would come to an end

And the belief that I could sway your affection to

match my heart's beat

Only to dread the witching hour

That broke the lock with no key.

Feature

Under by Tiffany Harris

If there is a such thing as under control

I've always played the star in that particular role.

Never knowing my best was less than expected.

We've been here 365 days and still not

connected.

We both preach about accountability but when

will there be a you and me?

Under expectations, under loved and un-true.

Seriously we've set a date to say I do!

Toxic isn't a trait in our world

Unfinished Business: Letters to a Broken Me

It's the food, air and the bed we emptily share.

Under-deserving and under expectations are all

that this has come to be.

When I said I loved you I thought it would be a

birth of a better me.

Guessing love is a term you use so loosely.

Verbal and mental abuse is all that I'm used to.

Underestimated and outdated

Wall portraits painted of how many times you've

told me I'm the one you've hated.

I've stalled and waited

Under water is how I've been breathing

Unfinished Business: Letters to a Broken Me

Knowing that it is bigger than you

Hell, I've just been grieving

Made in the USA
Columbia, SC
24 February 2022

56394923R00075